F. W. BLANCHARD

· ·

FIRST PRESIDENT
OF
THE HOLLYWOOD BOWL

A MEMOIR
BY

BEVERLY BLANCHARD NELSON
PAMELA T. LUNDQUIST

TRAFFORD

USA ▪ Canada ▪ UK ▪ Ireland

Cover Photo Credits (L to R)

City Hall: Security Pacific Collection/Los Angeles Public Library
Blanchard Hall: Security Pacific Collection/Los Angeles Public Library
Hollywood Bowl: HollywoodPhotographs.com

Note for Librarians: A cataloguing record for this book is available from Library and Archives Canada at www. collectionscanada.ca/amicus/index-e.html
ISBN 1-4120-8393-1

Printed in Victoria, BC, Canada. Printed on paper with minimum 30% recycled fibre.
Trafford's print shop runs on "green energy" from solar, wind and other environmentally-friendly power sources.

TRAFFORD
PUBLISHING

Offices in Canada, USA, Ireland and UK

Book sales for North America and international:
Trafford Publishing, 6E–2333 Government St.,
Victoria, BC V8T 4P4 CANADA
phone 250 383 6864 (toll-free 1 888 232 4444)
fax 250 383 6804; email to orders@trafford.com
Book sales in Europe:
Trafford Publishing (UK) Limited, 9 Park End Street, 2nd Floor
Oxford, UK OX1 1HH UNITED KINGDOM
phone +44 (0)1865 722 113 (local rate 0845 230 9601)
facsimile +44 (0)1865 722 868; info.uk@trafford.com
Order online at:
trafford.com/06-0148

10 9 8 7 6 5 4 3

IN MEMORY

OF

FREDERICK WOODWARD BLANCHARD

1864-1928

CONTENTS

ACKNOWLEDGEMENTS

My daughter and I would like to acknowledge the important people that assisted us with the completion of this book. We are both very grateful to everyone for their contributions and support.

First of all we want to thank our wonderful editor, Orlo Otteson. He took such an avid interest in the material and worked with diligence and integrity until the project was completed.

A special thanks to our talented graphic designer Kevin D. Parks, for taking our initial concept for the cover and turning it into a design that so beautifully captures the essence of Fred's life.

WITH LOVE AND THANKS

I'd like to thank my family individually and collectively for their interest in this project and for providing so much support.

First of all, I want to thank my daughter and co-author Pamela for her endless hours of research and writing and for encouraging me to tell Uncle Fred's story. This was a perfect project for a mother and daughter team and we greatly enjoyed our collaboration.

Thanks to my son-in-law (Pam's husband) Robert, for contributing photos and assisting with marketing and distribution.

Thanks to my son Ken and daughter-in-law Janet for the hours they spent researching genealogy records and a special thanks to Janet for diligently transcribing the family journals and diaries.

Thanks to my grandchildren Connor and Rachel for helping with genealogy research, showing so much interest in their family history and for continuing the musical legacy of the Blanchard family.

Thanks to my son Brad and daughter-in-law Myra for their meticulous review of the manuscript and helpful suggestions.

Thanks to my nephew Lester for his patience and the many hours he spent scanning the beautiful photos that are featured throughout the book.

Thanks to Ethel and Shirley for their integrity and for preserving so many of the Blanchard family photos and records.

Thank you to the Blanchard family for providing the wonderful material for this book.

And last but not least, I want to thank my husband Clyde for doing whatever was needed so diligently and right on schedule. He inspired me every day as we worked together in our office until the manuscript was finished. This book would not have been possible without him!

BLANCHARD FAMILY TREE

Top Row (L to R)
Elizabeth (Lizzie) Blanchard Hartwell, (Fred's sister)
Frederick Woodward Blanchard
Grace Hampton Blanchard, (Fred's wife)

Middle Row (L to R)
Dudley Blanchard, (Fred's son)
Clarence Blanchard, (Fred's nephew)
Augusta May Fox Blanchard, (Clarence's wife)

Bottom Row (L to R)
Harry Brownell Blanchard, (my dad, & Fred's great nephew)
Beverly Blanchard Nelson, (Fred's great, great niece)
Rachael (Helen) Nilson Blanchard, (my mother)

PREFACE

Pamela Lundquist: co-author

*J*n January 2002, my husband and I were contemplating a move from Northern California to Los Angeles—and exploring housing opportunities. While reviewing real estate listings on my computer, a pop-up advertisement appeared, showing the words "Beneath Los Angeles." I usually avoid these annoying ads, but for some reason I felt compelled to open this one. I opened it—and then froze in disbelief at the sight of an unforgettable image.

The image was a photograph of one of the most beautiful, expertly sculpted cemetery monuments I've ever seen. The top of the white marble monument held a circular design depicting the Hollywood Bowl. At its black base sat a sculptured weeping lady. The detail of the woman's hair, dress, and hands was absolutely exquisite.

I was impressed by the aesthetic beauty of the monument—but stunned by the name engraved across the top: *F. W. Blanchard*, a relative whose name and accomplishments were deeply familiar. He'd been part of our family conversation for decades, and his accomplishments had become forever embedded in our family history.

I stared at the photo for a time, pondering the odds of my coming across it. Of all the ads that daily pop up on the Internet, why did this one appear—at the precise moment I happened to be on my computer? And why did I choose to open it? I'd rarely opened one in the past.

Excitement and curiosity swept over me, and I immediately called my mother. As we talked, I knew that I must visit Uncle

Fred's monument, and I could sense that the event would move our lives in new and surprising directions.

Within weeks, my husband and I found ourselves standing in front of Fred Blanchard's monument, in the Hollywood Forever Cemetery, Hollywood CA. The surroundings were so beautiful and peaceful, and at that moment, as I stood in the Blanchard family plot looking at the familiar names, I felt a tremendous sense of family and community history, and I also felt a great responsibility to capture the memorable moments and outstanding achievements of Uncle Fred's life. And so the story begins.

Beverly Blanchard Nelson: co-author

After my daughter's phone call, in January of 2002, the two of us began talking frequently about Uncle Fred and his many contributions to the Los Angeles area.

From time to time, I would come across a book or magazine article that specifically mentioned how little had been written about F.W. Blanchard. Various articles stated that Mr. Blanchard had not received enough credit for the many important contributions he'd made throughout his lifetime.

It was a busy time in my life: I was studying, teaching music, and raising my family. Still, however, I would frequently wonder why there was so little published information about Fred's life and accomplishments. It bothered me.

Then one day, while reading an article about the Hollywood Bowl and the important role uncle Fred played in its founding—he served as the first President of the Bowl Association, then called the Community Park and Art Association—I was struck by a remark. The author noted that she was unable to provide more information about Frederick W. Blanchard, because his personal papers were unavailable.

Then I had a realization. I knew where many of Fred's important papers and records were stored. They were in my music library, at home. As the sole survivor carrying the Los Angeles Blanchard family name, I had inherited the family records—including scrap-books, bibles, tapes, diaries, newspaper articles, books, journals, and numerous photographs.

In June of 2004, my daughter and I, together with our husbands, attended a very special concert at the Hollywood Bowl. It was opening night of the summer season, and this inaugural concert was special—it celebrated the unveiling of the Bowl's new shell. It was an exciting evening for me, because it brought back so many wonderful memories from my youth.

As I sat there, enjoying all of the familiar sights and sounds of the Bowl, I thought about Uncle Fred, and I felt honored that I'd been entrusted by the family to preserve his most valuable possessions and records. And it was at this moment that the idea for this book was born.

I decided I needed to tell Uncle Fred's story, the story of a vision-ary man who seemed to have an idea a minute—a philanthropist, a cultural pioneer, a patron of the arts.

He was in the forefront of almost every notable planning program in the City of Los Angeles during the early 1900s. He was a prom-inent business and civic leader whose influence can be felt from Lankershim to Hill Street, from Cahuenga Pass to Hollywood, and from Broadway to the Bowl.

Fred's father is my great-great grandfather and this book is about Uncle Fred's life and the family members who supported him. As I started looking through the family papers and documents, I was surprised that I had so much material in my possession. And I was even more surprised by the number of documents and pho-tographs I'd received from various sources—valuable resources that I needed.

The stories in this book are ones I have either lived—or ones that have been passed on to me by my family members. I didn't know my Uncle Fred; he died in 1928. I feel, however, that I know him, because the family has never let his legacy die.

This book is dedicated to my uncle, *Frederick Woodward Blanchard*.

CHAPTER 1

....

THE EARLY YEARS

Boston

*F*rederick Woodward Blanchard was born in Millbury, Worcester County, Massachusetts, August 25, 1864, in the dark days of the Civil War.

Fred's great-grandfather, Samuel Blanchard (of French descent) had fought in the Revolutionary War, a source of pride to Fred, who greatly admired Samuel, perhaps because they shared similar qualities—determination, persistence, resourcefulness, intelligence.

In 1775, Samuel Blanchard married Susannah Tenney of Sutton MA, a marriage that produced nine children, including, Stephen, the oldest. Stephen in turn produced a son, John Sibley Blanchard, who married Harriet W. Putnam, a niece of General Israel Putnam—a prominent Revolutionary War figure. And from that marriage came Frederick Woodward Blanchard.

Fred grew up in Millbury. His father, a prominent businessman, owned and operated a large, successful shirt factory, but the family eventually moved to Boston, where John Sibley Blanchard took over the "Albany House," a hotel on North Beacon Street. At age 16, Fred held down a clerk job at the hotel.

Fred's uncle, Thomas Blanchard, perhaps the greatest innovator of automated woodworking machinery, invented the Blanchard lathe, which is still in use. This lathe allowed unskilled workmen to quickly and easily turn out identical irregular shapes. The lathe revolutionized the arms industry, and the technology was soon picked up by other manufacturing industries.

A prolific inventor, Thomas Blanchard once held twenty-four patents. In 1836, a fire ravaged the patent office, forcing officials to begin a new numbering system—to start over. We don't know whether Thomas's early records were destroyed in the fire. We do know that he held patent numbers three through nine in the new (post-fire) numbering system.

Stephen Blanchard, also an inventor, designed the shoe eyelet, one of those small but invaluable contributions to human well-being.

Uncle Fred came from a family of six. Siblings included:

~ Henry Wright

~ Nelly Marie

~ Annie Louise

~ Stephen

~ Elizabeth

John and Harriet, the parents, were dedicated to family life, and they valued education. Their move to Boston seemed to go smoothly, and Fred eventually applied for admission to the famed Boston Public Latin School (grades seven to twelve)—established in 1635, the country's oldest public school. Boston Latin requires an entrance exam, which would not have been a problem for Fred—he was exceptionally intelligent. While in Boston, he also studied music and launched a life-long interest in the nation's artistic life.

The Blanchard family enjoyed Boston's rich cultural offerings. Harvard College had been established in 1636, and by 1653 the city could boast a public library and a newspaper that was distributed throughout the colonies. Called the "Athens of America," Boston and surrounding communities spawned figures such as Ralph Waldo Emerson, Henry David Thoreau, Nathaniel Hawthorne, Henry Wadsworth Longfellow, and Louisa May Alcott.

After graduating Boston Latin, Fred and some friends sailed off for a European sojourn, an experience that strongly influenced

Fred's life course. He quickly took to the Parisian cultural life, and he especially reveled in the company of artists and musicians, many of whom gathered in coffeehouses to discuss their ideas and works. Fred, a dreamer who could make dreams come alive, began to envision an American cultural life that would promote artists and artistic achievement. He returned to America, and in 1882 he moved to the small city of Denver, Colorado.

Fred, a natural born musician—composer, pianist, organist—could even tune a piano, and he was said to have possessed the ability to perfectly tune the upper register.

In Denver, he soon met A. K. Clark, manager of a large music publishing house, and the two formed a business partnership they called Clark and Blanchard. Mr. Clark eventually asked Uncle Fred to join him in a Los Angeles business enterprise—a partnership that would endure until 1894. The prescient Fred had predicted that Los Angeles would become the largest city on the West Coast—and a great music and art center. He envisioned a Los Angeles that one day might be called the "Italy of the West."

Los Angeles

In 1886, at the age of 22, Fred settled permanently in Los Angeles and formed a partnership with J. T. Fitzgerald. Both men shared many of the same goals, and both were especially devoted to artistic pursuits. They founded a music company that sold pianos and other musical instruments. It was located in the retail district of Los Angeles, near Spring Street and First Street. The business soon became the leading music firm in southern California.

In 1889, Uncle Fred returned to Massachusetts for a special event—his marriage to Miss Marion, daughter of Mr. and Mrs. Isaac W. Tucker. On October 30, 1889, Frederick and Marion took their vows at the home of the bride's parents, in Alliston, Massachusetts. C.B. Tucker, brother of the bride, served as best man. Miss Lillian Tucker, sister of the bride, served as maid of honor. The Reverend, Dr. Quint officiated.

The bride wore a white gown trimmed with pearl ornaments. She carried a bouquet of "lilies of the valley." At the reception, approximately 200 guests were entertained by Baldwin's Orchestra, and the couple announced they would make their home in Los Angeles.

On July 20, 1891, a son was born—Dudley Tucker Blanchard. However, the marriage didn't last and in 1899, Fred and Marion divorced, an amicable parting. Marion and son Dudley settled permanently in Boston, but Dudley spent summers with his father in Los Angeles.

Fred Blanchard soon after arriving in Los Angeles

Fred at the Hotel Del Coronado in San Diego.

CHAPTER 2

....

BLANCHARD ART & MUSIC BUILDING
BLANCHARD HALL

*O*n May 1, 1899, the Blanchard Art and Music Building, located at 233 South Broadway, opened its doors to artists and visitors. Constructed by Harris Newmark, and planned and managed by Uncle Fred, the four-story building came to be known as Blanchard Hall—and it quickly turned into a flourishing arts center. Fred incorporated the business in 1899 and served as its first and only president.

The main floor contained commercial businesses and 140 small studios for artists and musicians. This floor also had two elegantly furnished public reading rooms, a gift from the Metaphysical Association. The top floor included a large exhibition space, as well as the Blanchard gallery—the first art gallery to be established west of Chicago.

The grand opening was a grand success. At the opening ceremonies, speakers noted the many unsuccessful attempts to establish an arts center in Los Angeles. But one news reporter of the day wrote that Blanchard Hall had all the earmarks of a successful venture—a prescient and accurate prediction.

An unexpected gift

In the afternoon hours, visitors viewed the "Old Masters Collection," on display in the Ruskin Art Club rooms, and the Paul de Longpre Flower Pieces in the art gallery.

About 9:00 that evening, guests were asked to assemble for a special

Blanchard Hall, 233 South Broadway, Los Angeles.
The first art gallery established west of Chicago.
Photo: Security Pacific Collection/Los Angeles Public Library.

What remains of the Blanchard Hall building in 2006. It was
severely damaged by the Northridge earthquake in 1994.

presentation. Frank F. Davis made a short speech and then presented Fred with an elegant gift—a solid silver and cut glass loving cup that stood on a mahogany pedestal. The gift, donated by the building's artists and musicians, was an expression of appreciation for Fred's devotion to the arts and to the City of Los Angeles. Fred accepted this honor in his usual modest and dignified manner.

Blanchard Hall soon became a thriving arts center. Music filled the building—recitals, vocal exercises, performances of all kinds. The Hall became a gathering place for prominent artists and musicians. But Fred was also sympathetic to young, struggling artists—even picking up a rent burden from time to time. He hoped for some return, however, and he usually received it, most often in the form of a good performance or a fine painting.

Many prominent artists and musicians rented studios in the Hall. Notables included Laura King, Florine Hyer, John Bond Francisco, and Francis Lewis Hord.

Fred finds a friend

In the 1900s, it was a popular tradition to adopt a mascot. Uncle Fred did not seek one, but he found one. It happened this way. One evening, in Blanchard Hall, a small eight-year-old boy approached Fred and took his hand. The boy, Clyde Tracy Hoag, announced that he loved music and that he wanted a job—he wanted to hand out programs to visitors. Fred leaned down and kissed the boy. He loved this little boy from the start; the boy had immediately touched his heart. Fred gave him the program job, and little Clyde performed admirably. A news reporter picked up the story, and soon an article appeared titled: *F. W. BLANCHARD HAS A MASCOT.*

The article identified the boy, and he and Fred formed an enduring friendship. Later, Clyde would take up the coronet. Fred provided unstinting support and encouragement—as he did for so many other young aspiring artists.

Blanchard Hall, a fine arts center, also hosted many civic activities and events. After leading a parade down Broadway during the California suffrage campaign, Inez Mulholland gave a speech at Blanchard Hall promoting women's rights.

In 1911, President William Howard Taft spoke to 1,000 people at a Blanchard Hall meeting organized by the Afro-American League. And in 1908, the resolutions for the Los Angeles County Good Roads movement were unanimously adopted by a convention held at the Hall. The Hall regularly hosted many other important meetings and gatherings. During the early twentieth century, Blanchard Hall was considered one of the most important public buildings in Los Angeles—along with other fine structures in the city, including the Federal Building, the County Courthouse, the Hall of Records, City Hall, the Shrine Temple, the YMCA, the Bible Institute, and the Trinity auditoriums.

Blanchard Hall hosted performances by the well-known Brahms Quintet, a group founded by Uncle Fred in 1910. Quintet members included: Oskar Seiling, first violin; Hermann Seidel, second violin; Rudolph Kopp, viola; Axel Simonsen, violincello; and Homer Grunn, piano.

After Uncle Fred's death, the quintet eventually regrouped. In a January 19, 1931, diary entry, Aunt Grace (Fred's wife) noted that Mr. Seiling had called to tell her that the Quintet was reorganizing. Aunt Grace responded by offering to give the group all of the Brahms Quintet music, her way of assisting the Quintet's efforts to continue without Fred.

Uncle Fred also provided leadership to the Gamut Club, an organization of professional musicians and prominent leaders in the Southwest arts community. Fred served as president of the Club over an eight-year period and he helped reorganize it. It was during his leadership at Blanchard Hall and his presidency of the Gamut Club that he helped bring numerous internationally recognized musicians, artists, and celebrities to Los Angeles.

Blanchard Hall still stands. It was badly damaged in the 1994 Northridge earthquake, but one can still see its main original characteristics. We hope the building will be preserved—and maybe even restored to its original state. Perhaps it might one day recapture its early glory—the site of splendid artistic and cultural achievements. Uncle Fred would love that.

ersonal Direction
F. W. BLANCHARD   **BRAHMS QUINTET**   BLANCHARD HALL
CONCERTS

The famous Brahms Quintet, (founded and directed by Fred), performed regularly at Blanchard Hall as part of the concert series.

CHAPTER 3

....

SOMETHING OLD, SOMETHING NEW, SOMETHING BORROWED, SOMETHING BLUE

*U*ncle Fred and Miss Grace Hampton exchanged vows on June 18, 1902, at the home of her parents. A newspaper report called it a "Hollywood wedding of much interest." It was, Fred firmly believed, a marriage that had been made in heaven, and he considered Grace the most beautiful woman he'd ever seen. A news report of the wedding described her as "a very handsome young woman of brunette type, and aside from the artistic temperament which has won her many admiring friends, she is possessed of a winsome personality."

Grace, an Illinois girl, had come to California with her parents just two years previous. Her father, a retired businessman, had purchased twelve acres of land at the intersection of Western and Sunset Boulevard, in the quiet suburban village of Hollywood, in a beautiful orange grove—and the family settled there.

Grace, who had studied at the Chicago Art Institute, had continued studies at Throop Pasadena, and her work was gaining some recognition. Grace's love of art and Fred's love of music seemed to nourish the relationship.

Fred, a proper fellow, arrived for the wedding at the proper time, and he found Grace more beautiful than ever. In keeping with a family tradition, she wore a single strand of 113 perfectly matched pearls borrowed from her soon-to-be sister-in-law, Elizabeth Blanchard Hartwell. I wore the same necklace at my wedding, as did my daughter, Pamela.

Grace Hampton (Blanchard) at age 13.

**A talented artist, Grace sketched this self-portrait when she
was a young woman.**

Grace's long flowing gown, made of ivory colored chiffon, was adorned with imported French lace, and she carried a bouquet of ivory and white roses, tied with elegant blue streamers.

The 3:00 p.m. wedding, conducted in quiet taste by the Reverend Robert McIntyre of Chicago, was blessed by warm Pacific breezes and inviting orange grove fragrances. An elegant lunch was served in the garden to the sounds of a string quartet. It was, all in all, a perfect day.

The bride and groom departed that evening on the "Owl" (a night train) for a honeymoon in San Francisco and Monterey.

Aunt Grace and Uncle Fred in the garden at the Hotel Del Coronado in San Diego.

....

CHAPTER 4

THE GREAT LIGHT WAY

*F*amily members all agreed: the events of May 1 had left Fred quietly and hugely pleased—indeed, they'd never seen him more pleased. His idea to electrically illuminate Broadway Boulevard had been embraced by the Broadway merchants. They had formed the Broadway Improvement Association, a group dedicated to advancing the *Cluster Lighting System*. And they'd selected their leaders: F. W. Blanchard, president; Glover P. Widney, secretary; and J. M. Schneider, treasurer. The plan called for the lighting to be installed first on Broadway—then on Hill, Main, and Spring streets.

Workers quickly began installing approximately 135 attractive iron posts on both sides of Broadway, staggering them on the curbs and placing four posts at each intersection. Each post held seven opaque bulbs—one large bulb encircled by six smaller ones.

The completed project seemed to add a touch of magic to the boulevard. A news article of the day noted, "When all the posts are up and the lights are turned on, the business sections of Los Angeles will be as light as day from sundown until midnight." The article went on to say:

> More than passing attention, that is well deserved, has been given the enterprising spirit exhibited by the business men and property owners of Broadway who believe in grit, and back it with generosity, and by their acts say to the city government and their competitors on other thoroughfares: 'Get in line; get busy; follow our lead; do things; put up your

cash; join in the movement to embellish, to brighten and to beautify Los Angeles.'

Praised as the most beautiful in the nation, the cluster lighting system was inagurated on Broadway with much fan fare.

Fred's drive to join aesthetic appeal with commercial success did not go unnoticed. Attorney John C. Mott, who presented the system to the city council, said:

> It does not require argument to fortify the assertion that money expended in making this city not only presentable but attractive is, in every sense, a profitable investment which will yield returns a thousand fold. Without discriminating as to other first-class streets of this city, it is apparent to all that Broadway is and will continue to be a prominent central thoroughfare, promenaded by thousands of persons day and night. All this may be said with equal force of other business streets, and we only specify Broadway because it happened to be the first to make a definite move in the direction of artistic public lighting. These great arteries of our much visited and rapidly growing city should, one by one, be made in outward appearance at least equal to the promenades and boulevards of European cities.

Opening night

In those years (c. 1905), parades were a popular form of entertainment. Everyone loved parades, and little six-year-old Harry (Fred's grandnephew) especially loved them. When his dad (Clarence) and uncle (Frederick) passed by, he'd wave his miniature American flag at them—and they'd wave back.

The inauguration of the Cluster Lighting System was scheduled for a Saturday evening. On Saturday, the family enjoyed an early supper, but little Harry couldn't touch his food—he was too excited about the upcoming parade. He carefully prepared a small sandwich and tucked it in his pocket—a little bite for later.

Upon their arrival in Los Angeles, family members quickly noticed the gathering crowd, and they sensed its anticipation. People peered from store windows and looked down from rooftops at the polished paved boulevard. Flags and streamers fluttered gracefully in the breeze, and colors emblazoned the street. The Japanese Lantern Festival gloriously crowned the scene. The parade would kick off weeklong festivities.

Darkness descended, and police cleared the street, calling "Tally-Ho"—one after another. Sirens sounded as Mayor McAleer made his way to the box that held the electrical switch lever. The mayor pulled the handle. The lights flickered for a moment—and then burst into full illumination. A great blanket of color erupted, a display that resembled a giant flower garden—all enhanced by the dainty Japanese lanterns.

Lights from the shops peeked through the crowds, and the Great Light Way sparkled as though basking in a noonday sun. The crowd delivered some thunderous cheers, and the Catalina Band led off the parade, followed by the mayor and friends, along with President Frederick Blanchard and other members of the Broadway Improvement Association.

The Hill Street Association float followed, a signal that Hill Street was next in line for the lights. Many "Tally-Hoes" and cheers greeted the float, which was decorated with hundreds of lights, all drawing energy from the trolley pole. The beautiful "Miss Broadway" adorned the float, wrapped in a magnificent coronation robe. Six ladies-in-waiting surrounded her, each holding a scepter with a device that symbolized the city's civic progress.

The Hill Street float had been designed by James Lang, Achille Bierel, and the Founding Association. It was followed by other floats, from other organizations: the Fraternal Brotherhood, the Y.M.C.A. Triangle Cadet Corps, the Los Angeles Military Academy Cadets. A colorful line of automobiles followed the floats, each decorated with flags, streamers, and flowers. The Schoneman Blanchard Military Band (my grandfather's band) led this entourage.

In the shimmering lights, one could see Japanese lanterns of every conceivable shape—all bobbing up and down, almost appearing to take flight. The Japanese folks were dressed in colorful native clothing—an elegant picture.

When the parade arrived at Temple Street, members could glimpse the County Courthouse. This marked the northern turning point. At Temple Street, parade members made a U turn to the north and marched back down the other side of Broadway—to Seventh Street. At Seventh Street and Broadway, the committee that organized the work, and the men who directed it for several months, were met by Col. J. B. Lankershim, who escorted them to his hotel for an informal supper.

But the festivities were by no means over. The Japanese proprietors still had many lanterns to sell at "just the right price." The crowd celebrated into the night, waving lanterns, flags, and streamers—until the Broadway lights finally shut down. Under the agreement with the City of Los Angeles Lighting Company, Broadway was to be illuminated only from sunset to midnight.

With the success of the Cluster Lighting System, Uncle Fred acquired yet another informal title: "The Father of the Lighting System in Los Angeles." Fred considered the lighting project one of his greatest achievements. It drew national attention, and it also drew praise from famed civic architect, Charles Mulford Robinson, who reportedly called the street lamps "the most beautiful in the nation."

This day marked the end of one era in Los Angeles history—and the beginning of another. Other lighting systems soon followed, more glowing tributes to another of Fred Blanchard's visions.

CHAPTER 5

....

CIVIC PROJECTS

*F*red loved his adopted city, Los Angeles, and he worked tirelessly to improve and beautify it. He brought a combination of talents to many civic projects: an imaginative yet practical mind, an artistic sensibility, and a dynamic set of leadership and executive skills. As president of the Central Development Association, Fred planned and initiated a wide range of projects, many of which endure to this day. He was, indeed, a master builder.

Good Roads

Uncle Fred simultaneously served as county chairman and vice president of the Good Roads Commission and as president of the Municipal Art Commission, which he organized in 1906. Which commission was most important to him? You could not tell, not even for a moment.

One day while being interviewed by reporters, Uncle Fred removed his hat, a gesture signaling that he was going to "stay a while." Fred and Aunt Grace frequently used the phrase "stay a while." It was a signature remark, a gracious greeting to friends that sent a message: "We're glad to see you; make yourself comfortable; stay a while."

This day, Fred (extremely skilled at interacting with reporters) wanted to deliver another "lecture" on the need to improve Los Angeles County roads. The old dirt roads, he thought, had long outlived their usefulness. "Tourists," said Fred, "give five million dollars a year to the economy of Los Angeles. Can we not use half of that to build roads that will benefit both them *and* us?"

Fred recognized that good roads were a powerful economic development tool. Merchants needed them to deliver goods to their customers. Farmers needed them to deliver crops and produce. Tourists needed them to fully soak in the Southern California sights. Fred further recognized that if Los Angeles County were to lead the way, others would follow: Riverside, San Bernardino, Ventura. Fred saw the need for a network of fine roads throughout Southern California—and he clearly saw the potential benefits.

On July 11, 1908, Uncle Fred, as county chairman and vice president of the Good Roads Association, called a convention to order in Blanchard Hall. He described the great progress that had been made in the Good Roads campaign. And he strongly urged the audience to continue working toward getting the $3,500,000 bond issue passed, although by this time approval had been virtually assured.

The convention endorsed the Good Roads campaign and unanimously passed two supporting resolutions. The enthusiasm and excitement within Blanchard Hall was palpable, as speaker after speaker pledged support.

The complexities, however, loomed large. How does one gain the cooperation of so many government agencies and civic organizations—and then maintain effective coordination? How does one keep the bond issue from becoming mired in politics?

Civic leaders decided to call a special election, and on July 30, 1908, the bond issue passed—as Fred had predicted. Supporters were thrilled, and they were eager to get started on a tough job: the construction of 307 miles of highways that would connect Los Angeles to every other community in the county.

Once again Fred Blanchard had used his leadership skills to turn dream into reality—to advance the common social good and to make life better for all Californians.

Municipal Art Commission
Uncle Fred saw community art as a vehicle for bringing all segments

THE "GOOD ROADS" RESOLUTIONS

Whereas, the Los Angeles county highway commission has filed its report with the board of supervisors recommending 307 miles of highways throughout the county for improvement, connecting the city of Los Angeles with every other city and town in the county and with each other and with the main highways of adjoining counties by constructing a solid rock macadam road with a protected top and providing for the construction of culverts and bridges of the most permanent type at an estimated cost of $ 3,500,000; and,

Whereas, the board of supervisors has ordered an election to vote upon the question of issuing bonds for that purpose, said election to be held on Thursday, the 30th day of July, 1908; and,

Whereas, the board of supervisors have, of their own motion, caused to be appointed an advisory committee consisting of the executive committee of this organization, together with the presidents of the Los Angeles Chamber of Commerce, the Municipal League and the Merchants and Manufacturers association, and Mr. William Mulholland, chief engineer of the Los Angeles aqueduct board, and said board have pledged themselves as a body, and each individual for himself, not to take any action contrary to the judgment of the advisory committee in the matters of letting contracts, confirming appointments or filling any vacancies that may occur upon the highway commission; now, therefore, be it

Resolved, by the Los Angeles County Good Roads association, in special meeting assembled;

First--That we do hereby unqualifiedly endorse the alignment of the roads as set forth, in the report recommended by the highway commission, and that after investigation we are satisfied that the estimates of the cost of said road construction have been carefully, systematically and accurately compiled, and we further believe that said highway commission is composed of men who are competent and thoroughly trustworthy, and will see to it that the funds are economically and satisfactorily expended, and that they are amply protected in doing the same, by the law under which they are constituted.

Second--That we believe this action should receive the unqualified support of every voter and taxpayer in the county of Los Angeles who is loyal to its best interests and should command their utmost individual and collective service from now until the close of the day of election, as this question is of paramount and immediate importance to the present and future welfare of this great county.

On July 30, 1908 the "Good Roads" commission unanimously passed two supporting resolutions at a convention held at Blanchard Hall.

of the city together— in a meaningful and purposeful way. He thought good art should be accessible to all, not just to the privileged few.

In early 1906, Fred organized an Art Commission and became its secretary. The Commission quickly gained official recognition and became a municipal commission, under the Los Angeles City Charter of September 5, 1911. Fred was named its president.

The following year, he served another term as secretary, continuing his efforts to bring art to wide public view. On August 2, 1922, Fred was again appointed president, and he served as president each succeeding year until his death in 1928—no small achievement, since his appointments were made each year by a succession of different mayors.

A couple of years after his death, the Municipal Art Commission prepared and hung a memorial portrait of Fred in the Art Commission rooms, in City Hall, to honor him and his contributions to community art endeavors.

In her February 20, 1931, diary entry, Aunt Grace took note of a meeting with the Portrait Memorial Committee in Mr. Colby's office. Mr. Lott was chairman of the committee at the time, and Mrs. Liscom was in charge of fund collecting. In a March 18 diary entry, Grace noted a meeting with a Mr. Maxwell to review the works of artist Max Wieczorek—the artist Grace finally selected to render Fred's memorial portrait.

The following week, Mr. Maxwell asked Grace to forward her favorite photographs of Fred. On April 22, Aunt Grace visited Max Wieczorek's studio to review the completed portrait. She remarked in her diary that the portrait seemed "very fine." A few days later, Aunt Grace and my grandfather took possession of Fred's portrait, but they held off presenting it to the Art Commission. It seems as though Aunt Grace wanted to keep it for a time, to have it all to herself for a while—an understandable wish. Grace never stopped missing Fred.

On December 6, 1931, Fred's memorial portrait was presented to the Municipal Art Commission by Blanchard family members and friends. It was, according to Aunt Grace,"a very beautiful ceremony."

As far as the family knows, Fred's portrait remained at City Hall until sometime in early 2000, when it was reported stolen. Although the details are sketchy, it seems the portrait was placed in storage after the 1994 Northridge earthquake, a time when City Hall was being restored. It disappeared and has yet to be recovered.

Uncle Fred's memorial portrait, by artist Max Wieczorek, was presented to the Municipal Art Commission December 6, 1931.

City Hall

In 1926, Los Angeles citizens began construction of a beautiful new city hall intended to reflect the city's ideals and its faith in the future. Again (no surprise), Fred took a leading role in the planning and building of this new city landmark, which opened shortly before his death in 1928.

Fred headed the committee that selected the inscriptions to be placed over the main entrance, and he also served on the committee that selected and developed the magnificent bronze entrance doors. The final design featured illustrations of important events in the city's history.

Uncle Fred also organized the effort to establish a permanent art exhibit at City Hall, a venue that he thought could also promote the work of local artists. He obtained and organized a small collection of paintings for the new building's opening.

The 1994 Northridge earthquake inflicted severe damage on City Hall. But rather than demolish this landmark, officials decided to restore the building to its original grandeur.

LA's beautiful new City Hall at night, 1929.
Photo: Security Pacific Collection/Los Angeles Public Library.

CITY HALL INSCRIPTIONS

"LET US HAVE FAITH THAT RIGHT MAKES MIGHT" LINCOLN

"RIGHTEOUSNESS EXHALTED A PEOPLE" SOLOMON

Fred headed the committee that studied and selected the inscriptions placed above the main entrance at Los Angeles City Hall.

City Hall's magnificent bronze doors. The design features
illustrations of important events in Los Angeles history.

Union Plaza Station

Uncle Fred was also an early advocate of an adequate railway passenger station, and, in his role as chairman of the Union Plaza Station Commission, he helped drive the development of the station. After city engineers recommended the Plaza site—northwest of the Civic Center downtown, across the street from historic Olvera Street—Fred helped city officials in their legal efforts to compel the railroads to build the station.

Following the resolution of legal and political issues, three major railroads—the Southern Pacific, the Union Pacific, and the Atchison, Topeka, and Santa Fe—began cooperatively constructing the station.

Architects John Parkinson and Donald B. Parkinson—the designers of City Hall and many other early twentieth-century Los Angeles landmark buildings—had been hired to design the station. They chose a combination of Spanish Colonial Revival and Art Deco design elements. The commanding scale of the building was truly impressive, as was the attention to detail. Uncle Fred died before its completion, but Union Station embodied his vision—high functionality combined with graceful and pleasing design.

Union Station opened in May, 1939, to great fanfare. Dedication ceremonies were conducted by Los Angeles Mayor Fletcher Bowron and California Governor Culbert Olson. As the key entry point to Los Angeles, Union Station soon became the main gateway to the city. Over the years, it has served as the backdrop for many films, including "Union Station," "The Way We Were," "Pearl Harbor," and "Bugsy." In 1990, the station was renovated and restored to its original grandeur.

Civic Center

Fred also greatly contributed to the development of the Los Angeles Civic Center, an area around City Hall noted for its architectural design and visual appeal. As president of the Central Development Association, and as a member of the Planning

Commission, Fred was heavily involved in the development of most early Civic Center projects.

Fred's contributions to Los Angeles civic life seemed limitless, and they earned him great respect and admiration. He possessed the keen business instincts and leadership skills that could drive a plan forward—and he kept his eye always on the future.

Moreover, although he enjoyed considerable wealth and prestige, Fred always considered the wants and needs of the less fortunate. He treated all he met with kindness and consideration, and his contributions truly earned him his exalted place in city life. No citizen was more widely admired and respected than Frederick Woodward Blanchard—and for good and substantial reasons.

CHAPTER 6

THE EXPOSITION AND AMERICAN OPERA

The Exposition

*T*he 1906 San Francisco earthquake and fire leveled the city and devastated its economy. But commercial life slowly improved over the years, and city officials eventually began formulating plans to host a 1915 world's fair—an event they knew would boost the economy. The proposed fair, to be called the Panama Pacific International Exposition, was intended to celebrate the completion of the Panama Canal and the 1515 discovery of the Pacific Ocean by explorer Balboa.

Several states campaigned vigorously for the privilege of hosting the Exposition, but President William Howard Taft finally selected San Francisco—for some very good reasons. The area's excellent coastal ports allowed sea travelers ready access, and European visitors could come through the Panama Canal, thus avoiding overland travel. Moreover, supplies for the fair could be more easily shipped by sea.

After the choice had been made, the members of the Boosters Club sponsored a special event at the Los Angeles Athletic Club. This formal affair, called the "Great Banquet," honored the 1915 San Francisco Fair delegation. One speaker, C.C. Moore, enthusiastically informed the audience that a "United California" had pledged its support for the Exposition—as had thirty-two nations and thirty-five other states. Guests at the main table included Uncle Fred and other prominent Californians: Los Angeles Mayor H.H. Rose; San Francisco Mayor James Rolph, Jr.; George

S. Patton; William H. Crocker; Mrs. Florence Collins Porter; and M. H. De Young.

San Francisco officials chose a site on the north end of the city—an area called the "mud flats." The flats were filled with debris from the 1906 earthquake, and city officials saw an opportunity to develop and reclaim 634 acres of prime property. The area today is called the Marina District.

Construction of buildings began, and citizens were soon introduced to some magnificent architectural design. The Tower of Jewels, 43 stories high, was adorned with thousands of colored cut glass pieces that cast shifting reflections in the Pacific breeze. The lighting schemes were a wonder to behold. A barge in the bay held fifty beaming searchlights that projected eight different light colors into the sky. The sight resembled the light displays that would later mark movie openings on Broadway Boulevard in Los Angeles.

Thousands of Americans trekked to the fair, many by automobile. The travelers discovered California's good roads, fine hotels, and cultivated citizens—and they gained even greater respect for their country and for the California vision.

Uncle Fred, Aunt Grace, and family members all attended the exposition, which covered seventy-six city blocks. On Los Angeles Day, the Schoneman-Blanchard Marching Band marched in the procession, together with my dad's high school band. My dad, Harry, then fifteen, served as the drummer. The trip cost each band member $65.00. For Harry the day was unforgettable; he would later describe the event as one of his greatest thrills.

The Exposition's Palace of Fine Arts, designed by noted architect Bernard R. Maybeck, was rebuilt in the 1960s and is known today as the Exploratorium Museum.

Fairyland—an American opera

In the year 1912, The National Federation of Music Clubs was making plans for its future. Mrs. Jason Walker, chairman of the

American Music Division, proposed that the Federation offer a prize for the best original American opera. Her committee suggested Los Angeles as a site for the opera's debut performance, since thousands would be traveling to the coast for the Panama Pacific International Exposition in San Francisco.

Mrs.Walker and Mrs. David Allen Campbell traveled west to discuss the matter. They met with Uncle Fred and asked if he thought Los Angeles would be willing to host the opera event. Fred, who saw the event as a great artistic opportunity for the city, assured his guests that he would be able to form a committee and develop a plan. He also agreed to serve as the committee's chairman. Fred loved music, but he also possessed dynamic leadership skills. He was well suited for the role.

The newly formed opera committee met and decided to invite opera compositions—and to award a prize of $10,000 for the best entry. Committee members set about raising prize money and other funds to cover production costs. The project was now officially in the hands of the American Opera Association of Los Angeles, under the leadership of Frederick W. Blanchard, president. Fred's visionary qualities, together with his pragmatic side, gave him the ability to effectively plan, organize, and execute these kinds of events.

The Opera Association decided to rely on volunteer workers, and members began developing a fund raising plan. The Association announced the opera competition and soon began receiving compositions. They placed each in a separate envelope, and then on award day opened each one by one in the presence of a notary. The decision was unanimous. The award went to composer Horatio Parker for his opera "Fairyland."

"Fairyland" opened on June 1, and audiences were drawn to its popular theme: the struggle for power in a mythical land. Performances ran through June 6.

Uncle Fred hugely enjoyed the Opera Festival. He loved opera, and he was himself a composer. He had written an Opera, "Cosita", The Daughter of the Don, that was performed in 1898 by an opera company in San Francisco.

Fred's gifts to Los Angeles civic and artistic life seemed to go on and on, year after year. He was one of those talented citizens who truly believed in advancing the well being of his city. His prominence was well deserved, and no history of Los Angeles would be complete without some description of his many interests and civic contributions.

Illustrated above is a copy of Uncle Fred's handwritten score of the Opera he composed "Cosita", The Daughter of the Don.

CHAPTER 7

....

GOOD MORNING LIZZIE

*M*y great-great aunt, Elizabeth Blanchard Hartwell (Lizzie), Fred's older sister, lived in Chicago with her husband, D. Edwin Hartwell, until his death in 1911—at the too early age of fifty-four.

Aunt Lizzie was born on January 6, 1858, in Millbury, Worcester County, Massachusetts. It was during their childhood in Boston that Lizzie and Fred began to develop a special bond that would grow and flourish throughout their lives. They shared many common interests including an immense love of music, art and culture.

Described by family and friends as a "formidable woman", Aunt Lizzie was independent, confident and strong minded. Perhaps these were some of the qualities that attracted a young man by the name of D. Edwin Hartwell.

Edwin was born in Philadelphia, Pennsylvania, December 23, 1856, the son of Edwin and Mary Butterfield Hartwell. Upon the death of his father, Edwin and his mother, Mary, moved to Nashua, New Hampshire. Edwin, an energetic, intelligent, talented young man, graduated Nashua High School and then went on to Bryant and Stratton Commercial School in Boston.

After completing his studies, Edwin resided at a hotel in Boston, for a time. The hotel was managed by my great-great grandfather, John S. Blanchard (Lizzie's father) and it was there Edwin met his future bride.

On June 10, 1880, at an 8:00 p.m. service, D. Edwin Hartwell and

Elizabeth Blanchard exchanged wedding vows. The ceremony, performed by Reverend William Bunton, took place at the Albany House, in Brighton, Massachusetts—an establishment the bride's father also managed.

The wedding was a lavish affair and a lively social event. Lizzie and Edwin enjoyed a wide social circle, and admiring friends showered the couple with many gracious gifts. Following the nuptials, a sumptuous banquet was served, and the bride and groom danced to the accompaniment of an orchestra. They departed shortly for a New York honeymoon.

The newlyweds moved to Chicago where Edwin went on to a successful business career. He rose through the ranks at Swift and Company, becoming secretary and serving as one of its most able executives. He possessed a pleasing manner, and he was admired and respected by his co-workers, who recognized his business skills and leadership abilities. He loved his home, and he loved to entertain—always with Lizzie close at hand.

A lover of nature, Edwin also appreciated art and music, and he was an accomplished pianist. Friends and family members admired his clear-headed thinking and his progressive views. He was a great American.

Following Edwin's death, Fred and Grace invited the widowed Aunt Lizzie to summer with them in Los Angeles. Lizzie accepted the invitation and, with Fred's urging, decided to settle permanently in Los Angeles. She and Fred began looking for suitable property on which to build separate houses, and they found it in the undeveloped rolling hills of the San Fernando Valley. They purchased sixty-seven acres of pristine property just east of the Cahuenga Pass, stretching from Lankershim Boulevard to the North and Pass Avenue to the South. In the spring of 1915 they began erecting their individual but adjoining dwellings. In that same year, Universal Studios began constructing a back lot on adjacent property, right next to the Blanchard land.

The purchase of this property was just the beginning of Lizzie's land acquisitions. Soon after moving to Los Angeles, she began

Fred's beloved older sister and family matriarch, Elizabeth Blanchard Hartwell.

investing in California real estate and purchasing stock in several promising young companies. Lizzie was extremely bright and possessed a keen business sense like her younger brother. It wasn't long before Aunt Lizzie became quite wealthy—spending much of her later life managing investments and funding her favorite charities.

Annie (Anne) Louise

Uncle Fred and Aunt Lizzie's older sister, Annie Louise, and her husband, Marshall H. Wells, often visited Fred and Lizzie in Los Angeles for extended periods. Over the years, Marshall and Annie acquired many Los Angeles friends, and they greatly enjoyed their times with their West Coast friends—and of course with Fred and Lizzie.

In the summer of 1912, Uncle Fred made plans to visit Panama—and to take Grace and Annie with him. His purpose was two fold. The first related to business. Uncle Fred, always interested in new ventures, wished to investigate potential business opportunities that would ensue with the opening of the Panama Canal. The trip was essentially a fact-finding mission, and it was supported by Los Angeles City officials.

A letter from Los Angeles Mayor George Alexander, dated September 10, 1912, stated: "The bearer of this letter, Mr. F. W. Blanchard, is one of the distinguished public spirited citizens of Los Angeles. He is visiting the Isthmus of Panama to gather information relative to the progress of the work."

Fred had another reason for visiting the Central American country. Marshall Wells, Annie's husband, had been working and living in Panama for a year-and-a-half. He owned shares in the Byano River Lumber Company, and he was an important manager in this company—which owned 115,000 acres of timberland, a railroad, and several steamships. The company was building mills in Panama, preparing for the Panama Canal opening and the lumber marketing opportunities that would open up.

After a wonderful interlude in Panama, Uncle Fred, Aunt Grace,

Fred and Lizzie's older sister, Annie Louise Blanchard Wells, is buried next to Uncle Fred at the Hollywood Forever Cemetery.

and Annie returned to Los Angeles, feeling good about their time with Marshall. He had greatly enjoyed the visit and seemed in good health. Then suddenly in November 1912, just two months after their return, they received news that Marshall had died of malaria—in the American hospital in Ancin. He was only sixty-two. Following Marshall's death, Annie lived with Aunt Lizzie on and off for the next thirteen years. Annie died on Aug 21,1925. She is buried in the family plot, next to Fred, in the Hollywood Forever Cemetery.

Fred and Lizzie's house construction projects, which began in 1915, were finally completed two years later. They moved into their mansions located at 3215 Hollywood Way (now known as Barham Avenue) in 1917. It would be an understatement to say the homes were impressive. A guarded gatehouse stood at the entrance to the estate, and a beautifully landscaped winding path took visitors to the top of hill—to the mansions. A vine covered Pergola connected the homes, and a natural spring, at the bottom of the hill, provided water.

Fred and Lizzie shared a tennis court, a water garden, and a grotto—together with acres of beautifully landscaped grounds, where colorful peacocks freely roamed. Movie studios used the grounds for film locations. Several of William Boyd's Hopalong Cassidy movies were shot on or near the property.

Lizzie's mansion, the largest, with twenty rooms and fourteen bathrooms, allowed her to entertain and host her friends and relatives, many of them from Chicago and the East Coast. Aunt Lizzie's music room contained a beautiful pipe organ, a church instrument that had been constructed in nearby Van Nuys. The room, which also contained a beautiful grand piano, was the site of many parties and family gatherings—of many sing-a-longs and jam sessions.

Uncle Fred and Aunt Grace's residence contained sixteen rooms, and it served as a great retreat for their creative and cultural endeavors. The quiet, natural setting lent itself well to Aunt Grace's painting pursuits. And it was in these surroundings that Fred dreamed some of his biggest dreams—and then formulated the

Uncle Fred and Aunt Lizzie's North Hollywood property as it looked in 1910. Barham Avenue (then known as Hollywood Way) running east and west with Cahuenga running north and south.

Same view of the Blanchard property as pictured above, taken after the Mansions were built between 1915-1917.

Uncle Fred and Aunt Grace's Mansion.

The Blanchard homes picturing the Redline shelter and guardhouse in the forefront.

Aerial photo of the Blanchard mansions

located at Barham and Cahuenga.

Fred and Lizzie's mansions were located at 3215 Hollywood Way, (now Barham) in North Hollywood.

The entryway in Aunt Lizzie's home.

Aunt Lizzie's music room had a beautiful pipe organ and grand piano.

Aunt Lizzie's dining room.

Aunt Lizzie's breakfast room.

Uncle Fred and Aunt Grace's breakfast room.

A guest bedroom in Aunt Lizzie's home.

Uncle Fred and Aunt Grace's bedroom.

The tennis court shared by Aunt Lizzie and Uncle Fred.

A BBQ, fireplace and water well located at the far end of the tennis court.

Aunt Lizzie enjoying a perfect Southern California morning on her balcony.

Aunt Lizzie getting into her car after visiting with friends.

plans that would bring them to life.

Looking back, I believe Aunt Lizzie and Uncle Fred built the homes primarily for family enjoyment. When Uncle Fred died, my grandparents moved in with Aunt Grace. And when my parents were constructing our family home in Westwood, we moved into Aunt Grace's house for a time.

Family members enjoyed many happy days in the "Big Houses," a term I coined when I was just a little girl. I vividly remember a Halloween party at the two houses. I remember the colorful costumes, the delicious snacks, and, most of all, the scary home movies—written, directed, and produced by my Uncle Dudley.

My parent's wedding was held in Aunt Lizzie's music room, and we always had Christmas Eve dinner at Lizzie's home, an event that included visiting cousins from Arcadia and Santa Barbara. I can't remember the details—I was too young—but my dad said it was always a spectacular evening, replete with a dinner fit for royalty.

My dad gave me my first tennis lessons on Lizzie and Fred's tennis court, and I remember a special birthday party on that same court, with many childhood friends in attendance.

The two mansions sat at the top of a hill. At the bottom of the hill, a Red Line streetcar passed through the property. When the county requested an easement to install the tracks, Fred readily agreed—but with one condition. He insisted on the construction of a shelter that would protect waiting passengers from the elements.

My dad told me a story about the "Big Houses" that sticks in my mind—and that reflects the love of home and family that Fred possessed. Fred and Lizzie, the two youngest of six children, were always very close. Fred liked to ride the streetcar into Los Angeles, and each morning on his way down the hill, as he passed Lizzie's home, he would call out, "GOOD MORNING LIZZIE." He didn't expect a response. It was just his affectionate way of saying, "I love you dear sister. "

Aunt Lizzie

After an extended illness, Aunt Lizzie died in her home on January 20, 1932—her nurse, Mrs. Gee, and some loving relatives by her side. Aunt Grace recorded details of the funeral in a diary entry. The funeral was held in Lizzie's beautiful music room, January 22, 2:30 p.m. The ivory walnut casket was placed in front of the large music window, and it was surrounded by flowers, including the family's flowers—a blanket of roses, lilies of the valley, and orchids. Dr. Crosser, Lizzie's pastor officiated. Mr. Allen served as organist and Mrs. Badnock sang "City-Four Square" and "Somewhere."

My grandfather, Clarence, stayed busy during those two days, attending to funeral events and other matters. He was close to both Fred and Lizzie, for his father, Henry Wright was their older brother.

Following the funeral, my grandparents boarded a 5:00 train and accompanied Lizzie's body to New Hampshire. She was buried next to her husband, D. Edwin Hartwell. Everyone missed her so very much. She was truly the family matriarch.

The two magnificent mansions remained standing on the hill, overlooking the Cahuenga Pass, until the mid-1960s. Some faraway observers claimed that they could occasionally see faint flickerings of light coming out of the houses. And they speculated that Fred and Lizzie had perhaps returned for a short visit—were perhaps spending an evening in their beloved family homes.

The mansions and the property were eventually acquired by Universal Studios (MCA), and the property is now owned by NBC/Universal. The homes no longer stand, but my recollection of them lives on, indelibly imprinted on my memory.

CHAPTER 8

....

HOLLYWOOD BOWL

*a*s the youngest member of a prominent musical family, my music education began at an early age. Dad and I would sit on the piano bench together, and he would teach me little tunes, passing on a love of music and keeping an unspoken promise: to continue the work that Uncle Fred had begun—contributing, teaching, sharing the gift of music.

Concert attendance was an important part of my music training, and I fondly recall evening concerts at the Hollywood Bowl, performances that Aunt Lizzie called "music under the stars." Uncle Fred firmly believed that an appreciation for good music could and should begin in the early childhood years.

The "music under the stars" tradition possesses a long, rich history. In ancient Greece, actors performed in amphitheaters—in Hollywood Bowl-like settings. Early European minstrels roamed the streets and fields, singing their songs. And early American parks were populated with bandstands; World War I concerts in these parks helped raise money for the war effort. At a time of unrest in Boston, Patrick Gilmore organized concerts he called "Peace Jubilees," which reportedly were heard by thousands and helped calm the city.

Uncle Fred firmly believed that good music enhanced the life and livability of a city. It had the power, he thought, to "soothe souls," and he had a musical vision. He wanted to breathe music into the Hollywood landscape, and he wanted *all* Angelenos to have access to good music—to be able to congregate under the stars and collectively enjoy beautiful music.

Bowl founders

The Bowl idea was conceived by a group of civic-minded men and women, active in the area's artistic and business communities. Dr. T. Percival Gerson, a physician, Dr. H. Gale Atwater, a dentist, and Christine Wetherill Stevenson, (heiress to the Pittsburgh Paint Company fortune), organized an August 12, 1918 meeting that led to the formation of the Theatre Arts Alliance.

Differences of opinion about the Bowl's purpose eventually surfaced. Two prominent businessmen then stepped in: F. W. Blanchard, president and C. E. Toberman, vice-president. Mrs. Artie Mason Carter, secretary provided strong leadership—promoting the project, raising money, and developing plans for a series of symphonic concerts.

Music for everyone

Early debates about the Bowl's purpose focused mainly on one issue. Should the Bowl performances be for the many—or just for the privileged few? The democratic idea prevailed, and board members and patrons agreed that the Bowl and the music should be a gift to all community members. They fully subscribed to one of Uncle Fred's favorite slogans: "Popular prices will prevail." To this day, the Bowl adheres to Fred's vision: one can still purchase a Bowl ticket for a dollar.

In the early years of the Bowl, the least expensive ticket cost twenty-five cents—and it remained twenty five cents for many years. In the early twentieth century years, social reform movements were afoot, and some reformers saw music as a way of promoting sound morals and virtues. For many, music was thought to have certain magical powers—perhaps the power to awaken the virtuous inner souls of all citizens. Some reformers saw music as a self-improvement tool, even a community improvement tool. Could the Bowl make Los Angeles a better place? Could Bowl music perhaps make Los Angeles a more virtuous place?

Sometime in 1919, actors staged a Shakespearean play in Beechwood Canyon, a natural amphitheater, and to great surprise, the performance turned out 20,000 playgoers. This event prompted Bowl visionaries to ask themselves a question: Is there not another canyon in the Hollywood Hills—another natural amphitheater that would hold the Bowl? The answer was yes. And after three weeks of searching, H. Ellis Reed and his father found it.

The Theater Arts Alliance acted and for $47,000.00 bought fifty-nine acres in an area called Bolton Canyon, near Cahuenga Pass, just a half-mile from the small town of Hollywood.

The canyon's acoustics were remarkable. From the center of the dell, one's voice could be heard at the top of the hill, a quarter-mile away. Musicians trooped to the site. The well-known violinist, Leopold Godowsky Jr., came with his Guarnerius violin—and was absolutely amazed. Singer Ernestine Schumann-Heink tested the acoustics—and could not believe the sound. Alfred Hertz, conductor of The San Francisco Symphony, was hugely impressed.

In earlier centuries, the Bowl site had been a meeting place for Indian tribes, who named it "place of the mountain." The Shoshones, a peaceful tribe, had visited the area as early as 1770. The site, on the west side of Cahuenga Pass (named after Chief Cahuenga), may have served as a Shoshone refuge. Legend has it that evening Pacific breezes still carry the sounds of tribal chanting and dancing. And Chief Cahuenga and family were reportedly converted to the Catholic faith within the confines of the little dell.

Uncle Fred thought the site ideal. It was within walking distance of most homes in the area—Can you imagine that today!—and only a half-mile from downtown Hollywood (population 5,000). Most Angelenos could reach the site by automobile; tourists and commuters could ride the Red Car Railway system. The temperate climate allowed for year around outdoor concerts, and men could simultaneously participate in two pleasures: listening to music and smoking cigars. Children could play in and around the site's trees.

In 1920 the Theatre Arts Alliance was reorganized into the

Community Park and Art Association—Frederick W. Blanchard, president. Charles Edward Toberman was named vice president; Artie Mason Carter was appointed secretary.

This was an exciting time for Fred. He saw a dream coming into focus, part of a vision he'd long held of a "New Italy," filled with high quality, affordable cultural offerings—and accessible to all. Uncle Fred never strayed from his slogan: "Popular prices will prevail." For Fred, the Bowl was for all the people—without exception.

Charles Edward Toberman, a successful real estate developer, handled the land dealings. He too had a dream—to create an "Oberammergau," a performance site similar to those in Germany. Toberman owned land along the rim of the canyon, and he donated this property to the Association—his way of helping maintain the pristine quality of the site. Mr. Toberman generously contributed time and money to the Bowl project; he was a true arts advocate and patron.

Mrs. Artie Mason Carter was also a driving force in the Bowl development. She had studied piano in American conservatories and in Vienna with renowned teacher Theodor Leschetizky, who had mentored some of the greats— Paderweski, for example, and Schnabel, known for his editing of Beethoven sonatas, which I have studied. Mrs. Carter's husband, a physician, strongly supported his wife's Bowl activities.

It is still exciting for me to read about the Hollywood Bowl—and about its officers, patrons, and activities. I admire the early Bowl founders and the fine and effective qualities they brought to this cultural development.

I've been involved in volunteer work all my life. I served for a time on the board of directors for the "Gina Bachauer International Piano Competition," held in Salt Lake City. I considered it an honor to serve on this board. I had previously served as president of the Utah Music Teachers Association, a member of the national organization.

I truly love to watch young people develop their musical talents. And I think my music experience has given me the ability to truly feel the joy that Bowl founders must have felt—as they saw a dream taking shape. As I think about these cultural pioneers—and especially about Fred's life—I think about their generosity, their dedication, their unselfish service. My respect and admiration for them knows no bounds.

"Bowl talk" has circulated in my family for years—across generations. My dad would tell me about the Bowl and the performances, and I remember him saying, "Bev, the Bowl was a very bright accomplishment. Music under the stars is so symbolic."

In 1921 the Blanchard family attended the first Easter sunrise service conducted at the Bowl. My dad said the chorus performance was absolutely breathtaking. A news article at the time described the day this way:

> When the Easter sun rose and faintly flushed the Cross far up on the Bowl's slope in 1921, thousands of men, women and children Easter sunrise pilgrims from all Southern California, lifted their voices joyously in praise of Him who made the Bowl, and thus established a tradition now dear to Hollywood.

The Fourth of July concerts were also spectacular, and they remain a Los Angeles tradition. The annual Christmas program featured a tall lighted Christmas tree—the only light in the Bowl. The Community Chorus would sing Christmas carols, and the audience would join in.

As the Bowl development plans moved along, founders decided they needed a bank loan to support their activities. After some discussion, bankers allowed that they could lower their loan standards for a project aimed at the "masses." Their use of the term "masses" riled Fred. The so-called "masses" had greatly supported the Bowl idea, and Fred and other board members refused to lower *their* standards—and cut the symphony by half.

Fred never lost his humanistic spirit. In his view, the Bowl belonged to "the people," and it was finally the people who would carry the torch to victory. Uncle Fred never lost sight of the big picture. He worked tirelessly to develop the Hollywood Bowl.

One favorite story says much about Fred's dedication to the Bowl—and about his own aesthetic sensibility. Fred, a fastidious man, and Bowl President, objected to the bare, dusty, unattractive entrance areas to the Bowl. One afternoon, he and some energetic volunteers showed up with hundreds of red geraniums in hand, which they promptly planted—greatly beautifying the areas. Fred loved the Bowl, and his Bowl work was obviously a labor of love.

In 1921, funding was still a problem, but a break was just around the corner. Some young Hollywood High School actors had staged a performance of Shakespeare's "Twelfth Night" at the Bowl. The high school had purchased an electrical switchboard, which it later donated to The Bowl. To show their appreciation, the management invited the Hollywood High School to hold their graduation ceremony at the Bowl, a tradition that continues to this day.

The founders kept steadily pushing their dream along. They wanted to establish an outdoor park and arts center that would entertain and inform all the people. They predicted that Hollywood would one day contain a large diverse audience, and they hoped that the Bowl would help develop community spirit. They wanted to involve the entire community.

Bright yellow banks

Bowl founders had this thought: since the Bowl was intended for the "people," perhaps the people would help with fundraising. The Bowl Association produced thousands of bright yellow pasteboard "banks," little receptacles that could take coins. These banks were distributed to stores, financial institutions, grocery stores, cigar stands, theaters—anyplace that citizens might be inclined to donate. And donate they did.

Tourists also pitched in and took the banks back to their hometowns. Hollywood High School students distributed the banks and then collected the offerings. A Boy Scout sent $100.00 from France. The entire Hollywood community volunteered services, including Business people who donated their time to serve as ushers. And all these efforts led to $10,000 of funding. The "people" were indeed making the Bowl their own.

Money! Money! Money!

Board members continually raised a familiar cry: "How can we raise the money?" The board would make a mortgage payment, and then some other expense would pop up. Fundraising seemed as though it would be an ongoing troublesome problem. But one special fund raising idea changed the course of Bowl history.

After analyzing their financial position, members of the Bowl Association decided to stage a special fundraising concert. They hoped to acquire outright ownership of the Bowl, and they informed the bankers of their scheme. At a special concert, they would ask the audience for pledges and then literally burn the mortgage contract in full view of the audience—before their very eyes. The bankers went along with the idea, and the stage was set.

Concert night began with "Schubert's Unfinished Symphony," and at intermission, Uncle Fred and Artie Mason Carter took the stage and presented the Bowl's financial problem to the audience. Mrs. Carter then held the mortgage papers high, and Uncle Fred symbolically set them afire—to the lively accompaniment of the orchestra. Fred then asked for pledges.

It was an historic moment for the "people," and they responded with great pride and generosity. They made their pledges, one after the other, and they truly made the Bowl their own that evening, which ended with the playing and singing of "The Star Spangled Banner." It was a night that would be long remembered, and it was a night that would benefit music lovers for many years to come.

In June of 1924, the Board approached Los Angeles County Officials and proposed that the Bowl be deeded to the Community Park and Art Association—that it be turned over to the County. The timing was good, since the Community Park and Art Association books were then in the black. Founders closed the books on the Association and created a new corporation called The Hollywood Bowl Association. They leased the Bowl to this new association for 99 years, with an option to renew for another 99 years. Annual rent—one dollar.

In October of 1924, the Bowl property was formally handed over to the County of Los Angeles, ensuring that the property would endure as a cultural center for all the people.

One of the many fundraisers held at the Hollywood Bowl.

Something for all people

Over its eighty six-year history, the Bowl has hosted an astounding variety of performances—operas, plays, children's choruses. Great symphony orchestras have performed at the Bowl—and great artists: Jose Iturbi, Marion Anderson, Lilly Pons, Louis Armstrong, Duke Ellington, Igor Stravinsky, Ingrid Bergman, Arthur Rubinstein, Frank Sinatra and the Beatles have all graced the Bowl. The Paul Whiteman orchestra can be added to the list—my dad tuned his pianos. The Bowl's beautiful outdoor setting, the brilliant acoustics, and the enthusiastic audiences have charmed and captivated performers for years.

And let us not forget the children—they are the Bowl's future. The Bowl has also provided a venue for budding musicians to showcase their talents on Young Artists Night. Over the years, children have given free concerts, sold tickets, and contributed in many other ways.

So the story of the Bowl is not the story of a handful of wealthy philanthropists creating a plaything—it is the story of Los Angeles people working together to create a lasting musical institution. The greatest honor we can bestow on these early contributors is simply to remember them and to praise their work.

On opening night, June 25, 2004, the Hollywood Bowl celebrated a special event—the unveiling of the new concert shell. I attended that event, and as I looked around at the crowd, I couldn't help but think about Uncle Fred and the other founders—and I couldn't help but ponder the rich tradition they had established. I recall my dad telling me about Uncle Fred's enthusiastic anticipation of the new season's program offerings. He attended every concert, until ill health finally limited him. But even after his passing, the family could still feel his presence at the concerts; they could still see him enjoying the performances and cheering everyone on.

Each opening night is special, but this 2004 opening symbolized a rebirth of the Bowl. As I sat there, and as music began to fill the air, I too could feel Fred's presence. I could see him sitting in his usual seat, front and center, enjoying every note and chord. I knew how much he would have enjoyed this special evening. But one thing would have pleased him most—eighty-three years after the first Bowl concert "the people" were still listening to "music under the stars".

A night concert at the Hollywood Bowl in 1933. The Bowl shell was designed by architect Lloyd Wright.

CHAPTER 9

....

GRANDFATHER

*C*larence William Blanchard, my grandfather, was born October 9,1870, in West Millbury, Massachusetts. He was the only son of Henry Wright Blanchard and Annie E. Bowles Blanchard—and also Uncle Fred's favorite nephew. Clarence spent his school days in Boston, and he spent enjoyable childhood hours working in Uncle Fred's music store, learning to tune pianos and enjoying the company of a good and kind uncle.

Uncle Fred left Boston in 1882 and eventually landed in Los Angeles, where he and his partner, James T. Fitzgerald, opened a music store on Spring Street. Clarence soon followed, and Fred put him to work tuning pianos.

Fred also hired a salesman, Harry Schoneman, who played violin, and with whom Clarence formed a friendship. The two joined forces with Emmet S. Peak, a cornet player, and formed a musical-comedy team—Grandfather serving as chief comedian.

But as often happens in show biz, conflict erupted. Fred felt that the late night gigs were causing Harry and Clarence to sleep on their day jobs in his music store, and he gave them an ultimatum—quit the band or quit the job. They chose the latter. And thus was born the Schoneman-Blanchard Orchestra and Dance Band. My grandfather held down the piano position, and my dad used to tell me about his highly accurate rhythm—so accurate, he would say, that "his left hand was as good as a metronome."

The orchestra-band held together for more than two decades, competing with other popular orchestras of the day and playing both in Los Angeles and surrounding communities, even as far south as San Diego County. The Schoneman-Blanchard Orchestra played dance music year around, and it became a household name in the area. My grandfather and others later formed a military band, which played summer concerts at Redondo Beach.

In 1915 Clarence was appointed librarian of the Los Angeles County Band, which was specifically organized for the Panama Pacific International Exposition, in San Francisco.

Clarence retired from the music business in 1919, the same year he played at the Catalina Island Summer Concerts. He was a charter member of Local No. 47 and a member of its board of directors from 1896 to1897 and again from 1900 to 1911. He served on numerous committees in that organization, but he finally relinquished his membership on November 28, 1919.

Grandfather Blanchard then opened a piano repair shop, and he also found work tuning pianos for the major motion picture studios. His great sense of humor and his joviality won him many friends. My home movies wonderfully capture this side of his personality. He always took time to smell the roses.

Clarence was a solid family man. In 1896 he married Augusta May Fox in Los Angeles. Three years later my dad was born. He was their only child.

My Grandmother was a striking woman and without a doubt, the love of my Grandfather's life. To family and friends she was known as Gussie, but to me she was Nana. She loved animals (especially the family cat Peanuts), and throughout her life she rescued many abandoned animals and found loving homes for them. Gussie was the peacemaker of the family and always strived to keep the household running smoothly.

I remember on rainy days my grandparents would pick me up after school and Nana would always bring a warm blanket and a cup of hot chocolate for me. I'll never forget how cozy it felt all snuggled up on the back seat of their car. I loved them both very much.

My grandfather loved to go places and do things. He once chaperoned my grade school class on a field trip to a well-known Los

Clarence Blanchard as a young boy in Boston.

Clarence Blanchard was a well known musician and pianist.

The Schoneman-Blanchard Band performing in the "Prosperity Week" parade in downtown Los Angeles.

Clarence and Schonie played at the Catalina Island Summer Concerts.

My Grandmother, Augusta May Fox Blanchard.

Angeles area dairy. I saw my first Jersey cow that day. We toured the dairy and then we each were served a small cup of ice cream. I recall a picture of a movie star on the inside lid of my cup.

I have fond memories of that day and of my times with my grandfather. He loved children, and I later enjoyed many other trips with him. In the summer months, I would accompany him on his piano tuning jobs. He liked to ride the streetcar into Los Angeles. He was a true grandfather—so much fun, such a good friend. One day we rode the streetcar into Hollywood and went straight to the Hollywood Palladium—to see a rising young star by the name of Frank Sinatra.

My grandfather loved the City of Los Angeles, and the city loved him. He was a well-known musician and pianist, fondly remembered as "Blanch" by his friends and colleagues. Clarence Blanchard died on November 19, 1946.

Clarence "Blanch" Blanchard.

....

CHAPTER 10

TWO FUN LOVING COUSINS: DUDLEY AND HARRY

Dudley Blanchard: a dashing young man

*U*ncle Fred and his first wife, Marion Tucker, produced one child, a son, Dudley Tucker Blanchard, born on July 20, 1891, in Los Angeles.

Dudley, handsome and intelligent, was born into privileged circumstances, and he made the most of it. He went on to Harvard University and was expected to follow in his father's footsteps. But, as often happens, this young man began developing his own ideas about his future—ideas that didn't fit Fred's vision for him.

After finishing his Harvard studies, Dudley returned to Los Angeles and launched a career in the film industry. In the summer of 1916, he landed a job with the Jesse L. Lasky Feature Play Company, working as an assistant director on the silent film "The Lash." The film—starring Marie Doro, Elliott Dexter, and James Neill—was released on October 1, 1916. Dudley continued with the Lasky Company, helping turn out three more films: "Oliver Twist," "Freckles," and "The Jaguar's Claws."

After a four-picture run with Lasky, Dudley signed on with the prestigious Mary Pickford Film Corporation—an exciting time in an increasingly exciting business. In his first assignment—assistant director for the film "Rebecca of Sunnybrook Farm"—Dudley actually worked with luminaries Mary Pickford, Eugene O'Brien, and Helen Jerome Eddy. And it was at Pickford Films that Dudley met Edith Elizabeth Coulter, a beautiful young actress known in the film community as Tonnie Thomas.

Fred's only child, Dudley Tucker Blanchard.

The two became engaged, but their busy film schedules made it difficult to set a wedding date. At the time, Dudley was heading up the cutting department for the National Film Company and Edith was working for the Jesse L. Lasky Company.

So, one Saturday evening, Dudley took his fiancé for a drive through Hollywood. He had recruited a friend (an accomplice) to join them, and the three drove directly to the residence of a local minister—where he and Edith were married.

Dudley's marriage to Edith Coulter was short-lived and after they divorced, he continued to immerse himself in the excitement surrounding a budding Hollywood film community. But he had learned well from his father and he didn't forget his civic duties and his family legacy. He took a campaign director position with the Hollywood Bowl. In this position, he conducted the pre-season ticket drives for the Bowl, a job he'd previously held as a volunteer.

Dudley eventually remarried, and this marriage produced his only child, Richard Sawyer Blanchard. Richard inherited his father's good looks and high intelligence, and he too staked out a very promising future. He attended the Naval Academy in Annapolis, graduated Yale University, and earned a medical degree from Harvard Medical School.

Then while completing his medical residency in Hawaii, Richard died of cancer, at the young age of twenty-seven. His death was a heartbreaking loss for the family. Not only was a young and promising life cut short—the family also lost the last male of the Los Angeles Blanchard line.

Harry Blanchard: fashion plate of Broadway

Harry Brownell Blanchard (my dad) was born in Los Angeles on January 28, 1899. His parents were Clarence William and Augusta May Fox Blanchard. His godfather was Harry Schoneman, and Schonie, as we called him, became a familiar presence in the Blanchard household.

Music filled their home, Dad played drums, piano, and xylophone—and he was a natural. I once asked him if Grandfather had taught him piano, and he said, "No, I just picked it up." I also asked him when he had started taking drum lessons. But, again, no lessons—he just picked it up. At age twenty-five, he actually took some drum lessons from one of the best drummers in Los Angeles.

He began his drumming career in the basement (or cellar, as he called it), equipped only with two sticks and a board, but his parents soon gave him a drum set—they'd become aware of his innate talent. In grammar school (elementary school), little Harry would play his drums as the students marched out for recess. He also "drummed them out" at the end of the day. Dad explained that kids weren't in such a rush those days—more inclined to march out in an orderly fashion.

As a grammar school student, my dad also played the bells in the school orchestra. His teacher was amazed at how well he read the music. Well, at this point, he couldn't read music at all—he was playing by ear.

When Clarence and Schonie would have orchestra rehearsals, Dad would often be present—focusing especially on the drummer. This was about the time Dad's drumming career began to take off. In his last grammar school year, he was asked to play in a movie theater orchestra. It was a non-union orchestra. He worked every night and took home about $10.00 a week. The next day he would fall asleep in class, which distressed his mother, who questioned his musical ambitions.

But Clarence had decided that Dad was intent on becoming a drummer—and that there was no point in fighting it.

In high school, Harry played in both the band and the orchestra. In 1915, students could select classes of their choosing. Harry chose music appreciation, harmony, piano, counter point, orchestra, and gym—knowing that these courses would not lead to a diploma. But he didn't care: he was going to be a drummer, and he was not going to be deterred.

Harry Blanchard (my dad) as a young boy.

Harry's first assignment at Manual Arts High School was memorable: he played in a production of Victor Herbert's "Serenade." These performances were open to the public, and Dad was very proud to be member of the orchestra.

At this point, Harry had joined the musician's union. My grandfather had to post his bond, since Harry was under age. He then received an offer to play at Solomon's Ballroom for $25.00 a week. Imagine, Dad was only 15 years old— still a teenager, but playing professionally.

This same year, his high school marching band was asked to participate in the Tournament of Roses Parade and Rose Bowl game. Rain soaked the band members' beautiful white broadcloth uniforms, each of which had cost $65.00—a lot of money in those days. Dad said, "We had three problems that day: the rain, the mud, and the horses—we marched just behind the horses." His mother later dealt with the laundry issues surrounding the "horse problem." My dad possessed an innocent quality that allowed him to enjoy and appreciate even the simplest life experiences.

Prior to the Tournament of Roses event, Dad's high school band had performed at the Panama Pacific International Exposition— the San Francisco World's Fair. Several family members attended this event, including Clarence and Harry. On Los Angeles Day, the Schoneman-Blanchard Marching Band marched in the procession, together with my dad's high school band.

By this time, Dad was playing so well that Clarence asked him to join the Schoneman-Blanchard Dance Band and Orchestra. So Dad quit Solomon's Ballroom and went to work for his father at Redondo Beach.

In the meantime, Aunt Lizzie had decided that Harry should attend a university, and her choice was Harvard, in keeping with a Blanchard tradition. Aunt Lizzie worked hard on this college project, and just when it seemed she was making some progress, Harry would show up in an orchestra someplace. Lizzie persisted, but Harry won—he would be a drummer.

In 1919 Dad was invited to play in the Majestic Theater, an up

Little Harry was a natural born musician.

Harry in a school play in the San Fernando Valley.

Harry became a professional musician at the age of 15.

scale Los Angeles ballroom. But he then shortly returned to Solomon's—they needed both a drummer and a xylophone player. This meant another raise and an opportunity to make a valuable purchase—some silk shirts. As Dad told me, "You needed a silk shirt to be classy."

Dad spent one summer in Catalina, playing with a small band on the dock. As passengers approached, they were treated to a lively musical greeting. One afternoon, Aunt Grace and Uncle Fred met Harry there, and they were thrilled to see him. Uncle Fred would have preferred to see him away at college, but he understood talent. And he understood, too, that Harry was pursuing his dream—to be a professional musician, to play and perform. It did not escape Dad's attention (then a single man) that he was often in the presence of pretty girls. The Blanchard men always had a sharp eye for beautiful women.

Dad ultimately met Harry Jackson and played with his orchestra for about twelve years. They played the uptown clubs: The Wilshire, the Santa Monica, Jonathan's, and the L.A. Athletic Club. This was an exciting time in Dad's life, and he was also drawing down some big bucks. At one time, he was called the "Fashion Plate of Broadway."

Dad returned to the Majestic Theater for a time. Later he played at the Metropolitan Theater, and it was there that he met Eddie Peabody, one of the great banjo players of the time—and of all time. Dance bands were very popular through the Twenties and Thirties, and many musicians found themselves in a great place, able to play some of the fine spots around the country—and also able to make a decent living. When Dad recalled those times, his eyes would shine and sparkle.

Dudley moves out—Helen moves in

My dad and my mom, Helen, met at one of Hollywood's most renowned restaurants, the famous Pig 'N Whistle. During the Twenties, Hollywood Boulevard was the place to be seen—known for its magnificent movie palaces, including the Egyptian

Theater, right next door to the Pig 'N Whistle. The restaurant adjoined the theater, and it became a gathering place for stars—and I mean stars: Clark Gable, Cary Grant, Shirley Temple, Spencer Tracy, Loretta Young, Jane Wyman.

It was around this time that my parents became engaged. Dad was performing at the Pig 'N Whistle with his popular quartet, and my mother was working as a hostess, serving salads to the luminaries who patronized the restaurant. Mother was so beautiful she could have been a film star.

Her engagement ring had been purchased in Europe by Aunt Lizzie, who had given it to Dad, to give to his future bride. The couple was married in Aunt Lizzie's mansion.

Dudley and Dad occupied a bachelor pad in Laurel Canyon. After my parents married, Dudley moved out, and Helen moved in. I am Harry and Helen Blanchard's only child. The night I was born, Dad was performing at the Metropolitan, and I'm told that he dedicated a number to his new baby daughter, Helen Beverly Blanchard. From that day forward, for the rest of my life, till the day he died, my dad remained my best friend.

In the Thirties, every theater had a stage band. (Live music—what a treat!) Dad told me that the Metropolitan had a thirty-chair orchestra and that he made $168.00 a week working the Metropolitan, pretty good pay in the Depression Thirties. The Metropolitan was later demolished and replaced by the Paramount.

During this time, Dad also owned and operated a music store on Sunset Boulevard. He was well known as a successful proprietor and recognized as a fine musician. He stayed at the Sunset location for about a year and then moved the business to Santa Monica Boulevard in Hollywood. His store on Santa Monica wa called the Blanchard Music Company. It was located at 8161 Santa Monica Boulevard in the upscale Carmel Theatre Building.

Harry's stage career finally ended, and he joined the Navy, serving in World War II aboard the U.S.S. Detroit. This didn't end his music career: he organized and directed a small band on the ship. When he returned home, he carried on the family tradition.

He picked up his tools and continued to tune pianos for motion picture studios and film stars.

My Dad gave me an appreciation for good music of all kinds. He taught me to enjoy the small things, and he passed on his sense of humor. He also taught me to be kind and considerate, and I've always remembered his cautionary remark, "Remember, Bev, things aren't always as they seem." My Dad, Harry Blanchard— my best friend—died on March 6, 1983.

Harry Brownell Blanchard - "Fashion plate of Broadway".

Rachael Helen Nilson Blanchard (my mom).

Helen and baby Beverly.

Invitation to the opening of the Blanchard Music Company store located at 8161 Santa Monica Boulevard in West Hollywood.

Harry standing in front of his company car.

Store front of the Blanchard Music Company.

The Blanchard Music Company was located in the Carmel Theatre Building in the early 1930's.

The Blanchard Music Company store front as it looks in 2006.

Harry, Augusta and Beverly at Catalina Island.

CHAPTER 11

MRS. BLANCHARD—
DINNER IS SERVED

*U*ncle Fred's wife, Grace Hampton Blanchard, was known to the family as Aunt Grace. She was a lovely, charming lady with a contagious laugh that made us all want to join in. In a Jan 1, 1931, diary entry, she noted that we *all* went to the Rose Parade. Her use of the word *all* is significant—the Blanchard family was always together.

After Uncle Fred passed away, Grace moved out of their mansion in North Hollywood and bought a beach house on the Strand, at Hermosa Beach. It was the perfect place for her to rest and recuperate. The family visited her often and spent many enjoyable hours there. Aunt Lizzie and Aunt Grace spent much time together at Hermosa Beach—they seemed truly sisters at heart.

Pedro, Lizzie's domestic helper, also spent time at the beach with Aunt Grace. Pedro had come to California from the Philippine Islands, and he worked for Aunt Lizzie in her mansion from 1929 until 1932, the year of her death. Pedro then went to work for Aunt Grace and stayed with her for the next thirty-seven years.

Pedro had a wife and four children in the Philippines, and he dearly missed them—one reason he may have related to me so well. I liked Pedro—he paid special attention to me. He called me "Missy," and I would beg Aunt Grace to let me help Pedro serve dinner. But Grace would not allow this—it was against the social norms of the day.

Aunt Grace would summon Pedro from the kitchen with a buzzer.

Grace Hampton Blanchard was known to the family as Aunt Grace.

Aunt Lizzie and Aunt Grace out for a ride to the beach. The driver is Lizzie's chauffeur, Thomas.

Aunt Lizzie and Aunt Grace spent much time together at Hermosa Beach—they seemed truly sisters at heart.

Beverly, Augusta, Clarence, Helen, Grace and her cousins, visiting Grace's house on the Strand at Hermosa Beach.

As a young girl, I loved to push the buzzer button, and many years later I would watch my own little girl push the same buzzer.

Pedro stayed with Aunt Grace until the time of her death. In her will, she noted that Pedro was her loyal friend and devoted servant. He was 75 when she died.

I have so many fond memories of Aunt Grace and the good times we enjoyed as a family. She was always so gracious and thoughtful. One afternoon, in almost ceremonious fashion, Aunt Grace presented me with Uncle Fred's bible. It had been his grandfather's bible, published in 1843, and it contained, among many other things, a detailed description of Fred's funeral. I was so touched that Aunt Grace would trust me with this most prized possession. Aunt Grace passed away on October 3, 1969 and is buried next to Uncle Fred.

CHAPTER 12

THE WEEPING LADY

On Friday September 21, 1928, Frederick Woodward Blanchard—civic leader, arts patron, cultural pioneer, dear friend, and beloved family member—died in the Hollywood Hospital, after a four-week illness. Fred had given forty years of service to his adopted city, Los Angeles, and his passing seemed to mark the end of an era.

Uncle's Fred's funeral was held in the Wilshire Methodist Church, on Hobart Boulevard, October 3, 1928. Services had been delayed by the family so that Aunt Lizzie, who was vacationing in England, could return to Los Angeles—to grieve and to pay tribute to her beloved younger brother.

Hundreds of friends attended the services to pay their last respects to a man described as a "pioneer patron of Los Angeles music, art and culture, a tireless worker for civic ideals, a dreamer whose dynamic endeavors turned dreams into reality and a man whose name will forever be identified with the development of the city."

The flowers stood in a bank six feet high that stretched for fifty feet around the altar—a breathtaking sight for family members. The beautiful arrangements came from city officials, organizations, and friends. They came from those who had benefited from Fred's many philanthropic works and from those who had simply admired and respected him from afar.

In his eulogy, Dr. Willsie Martin noted that Fred "was a trailblazer, starting Los Angeles on its way to becoming the art center of the world, a dreamer who saw his dreams come true." He went on to say that citizens could only approximate the good that would come from his great work.

In another eulogy, Rabbi Magnin said, "We shall remember Mr. Blanchard as a good citizen first. We shall see Los Angeles rise from a rather sprawling area to one of compactness. This will come through the principles of planning laid down by Mr. Blanchard. A history of our city can never omit his name as one of our outstanding men."

The City of Los Angeles closed its civic and government offices for the funeral and cemetery services. The city prepared Resolutions of Condolence describing and acknowledging Uncle Fred's services to Los Angeles. An embossed copy was presented to Aunt Grace.

Leaders in the public, educational, business and social circles of Southern California served as pallbearers. The active pallbearers were E.T. Marks, W.R. Dickinson, E.S. Bogardus, J.J. Backus, Harry Lee Martin and C.E. Toberman.The honorary pallbearers were B.F. Bledsoe, L.E. Behymer, Harry Chandler, E. A. Dickson, J. Bond Francisco, Dr. Edward R. Kellogg, Stewart Laughlin, John Myers, Max Meyberg, John Parkinson, Victor H. Rosetti, R.J. Scott, W.P. Whitsett, S. H. Woodruff, Fred B. Kellogg, and N. C. Mason.

The funeral cortege included 100 automobiles. Uncle Fred was laid to rest in beautiful surroundings, in Hollywood Memorial Park, now called Hollywood Forever. The grounds are located at Santa Monica Boulevard, adjacent to Paramount Picture Studios.

Graveside services were brief and simple, and the picturesque setting seemed so appropriate for Fred. The expansive lawns, the tall palm trees, and the Hollywood sign in the background seemed to reflect the nature of the man. Fred's gravesite is surrounded by those of other Los Angeles pioneers and notables, including General Harrison Otis, founder of the Los Angeles Times, and businessman Charles Toberman, Uncle Fred's longtime friend and colleague.

Hollywood Forever is also the final resting place for many entertainment moguls and celebrities, including Cecile B. DeMille, Jesse Lasky, Mel Blanc, Marion Davies, Tyrone Power, Douglas

Fairbanks, Jayne Mansfield, Eleanor Powell, Peter Lorre, Faye Raye, Gilbert Adrian (celebrity fashion designer) and his wife Janet Gaynor, and Rudolph Valentino.

My daughter and I have visited Uncle Fred's gravesite many times, and we are always moved by the beauty of his monument. It was designed by famed architect Lloyd Wright, who designed the original Hollywood Bowl shell. The top portion of the monument depicts the Bowl and symbolizes Uncle Fred's important contributions as a founder, developer, and first president. At the base sits an elegant weeping lady holding a lyre. The sculpted detail of her hair, dress, and hands are absolutely exquisite.

Uncle Fred's monument holds deep meaning for the Blanchard family. The design incorporates elements from a Greek mythological story. The story goes like this.

The musician, Orpheus, son of Apollo, is given a lyre, a gift from his father. He plays so sweetly that even the wild beasts are tamed by his strains. He plays for his fellow mortals, yet even the trees and rocks respond to his musical charms. Eventually Orpheus wins the heart of his true love, Eurydice, and they marry.

One day, shortly after the marriage, while Eurydice is wandering with the nymphs (her sister companions), she is spotted by a group of shepherds, who are smitten by her beauty. They began chasing her through the tall grass. While fleeing, Eurydice is bitten by a snake in the grass—and she dies.

Orpheus, grief stricken, sings of his sorrow and resolves to find his wife in the Land of the Dead. He finds Eurydice, and he presents himself before the throne of Pluto and Proserpine, begging for permission to lead his true love home. His request is granted, but with one condition. He must not look back to see whether Eurydice is following him. In his excitement about the reunion, however, Orpheus looks back. In a flash, Eurydice is taken away and returned to the Land of the Dead. The grieving Orpheus is ultimately killed, and he joins Eurydice in the Land of the Dead, where they live together forever.

The family feels a strong attachment to this myth. We see Aunt Grace as the weeping lady in the monument, holding the lyre, which represents Uncle Fred's love of music. They see Fred and Grace once again together, next to each other in the Blanchard family plot. With them are Fred's sister, Annie Louise Wells, and my grandparents. My father's headstone sits next to his parents' gravesites.

Although Frederick Woodward Blanchard left this world almost eighty years ago, his memory and legacy endure. One of the funeral eulogies seemed to say it all.

> Today at the Hollywood Memorial Park, honors will be paid to one of the most gifted and best loved of Los Angeles citizens, Frederick Woodward Blanchard. The beautiful plot of consecrated ground, hallowed to the memory of so many of those most intimately connected with the progress of the Southwest, has been the scene of many sad and impressive ceremonies, but few of these have been so fraught with feeling as to touch the hearts of so great a multitude of admirers.

> The monument to this unselfish worker for higher civic ideals will not be confined to the burial ground where other Los Angeles pioneers sleep the sleep eternal. Nor will the flowers laid above a cypress-covered grave be the last tribute his memory will receive. Flowers that never perish are growing in the homes and institutions of the city he served for forty-two years devoted to its artistic betterment, and these are as immortal as the spirit that sowed the seed.

> Names pass away in the rush of the years hurrying along newer areas under the direction of younger hands and brains. Obelisks and gravestones tell little to a coming generation of the one that these loving devices would save from oblivion. It will not be long before those gathered here today, will like the leader they mourn, solve the last long problem of human destiny.

But the efforts of such lovers of their race and city as the man who was but yesterday a leading force in our civic and artistic life are beyond the touch of death or the taint of mortality. The work of Fred W. Blanchard will live as long as the Civic Center he took so large a part in planning. Not in the Hollywood Cemetery, but in America's noblest City Hall he has reared his most lasting monument. When the Hollywood Bowl vibrates with its starlight symphonies, his spirit is there. Whenever the Municipal Art Commission devises new means for beautifying our city, a seed he planted flowers again.

Though his name, save in the hearts of the survivors who knew him and valued him through personal contact, may in time be only a name to the curious seeking memorials of the past in a city's Valhalla, from Windsor Square to Dana Point, from Hollywoodland to Arrowhead, all through the Southwest beauty spots he devised and music and art into which he breathed the breath of life will testify to his unselfish citizenship and be an everlasting tribute to his uplifting labors. Names, indeed may disappear in the swift changes of an age on wings, but the work of such men as him to whom today a city pays the last earthly honors, are flowers of immortality.

Fred's monument at the Hollywood Forever Cemetery in
Hollywood was designed by famed architect Lloyd Wright,
designer of the Hollywood Bowl shell.

EPILOGUE

J was born into a family (immediate and extended) of extraordinary talented musicians. I was an only child, maybe a bit "spoiled," but, amazingly, I didn't seem to annoy anyone—perhaps my parents on occasion. My Hollywood childhood experience was special. I became star struck at an early age, and I confess that I'm still star struck.

My dad and my grandfather tuned pianos at the major movie studios, and as a child I would often accompany them, although I never knew exactly which day the visits would occur. We would leave for the studio about 10:00 in the morning, and we'd go directly to the sound stage. During one of these visits, as they were filming, my dad struck a match to light his cigarette, and immediately shut everything down. All hell broke loose, when the director screamed, "What idiot lit that match?" Dad, embarrassed, raised his hand, extinguished his cigarette and soon they began filming again.

One time, as we were leaving the sound stage, Dad noticed Jean Harlow returning to her dressing room. We hurried to catch up to her, and just as she was about to enter her room, Dad introduced himself, and she invited us in. Dad had asked for an autographed picture—for his little daughter. And of course she gave us one.

I especially liked trips to the Disney Studios with Dad and Grandfather. We would travel up a long driveway, and you'd have thought we were approaching a Southern mansion and estate. The green grass seemed to stretch on forever. The receptionist would usher us into the drafting room, and then I would sit on a high stool and actually watch the artists draw their cartoons (no computers in those days).

Dad would always say, "I'll be back in a while," and then he would go off and tune pianos. I was amazed that I could watch the artists draw the cartoons one day—and then later watch the same cartoons in a movie house on another day. A big part of our visit for me was the ice cream treat afterwards.

I would often accompany Dad on his piano tuning trips to the Orpheum Theater, on South Broadway, in the Los Angeles historic theatre district. After the piano tuning was completed, we would stay for the rehearsal. One afternoon we watched Tommy and Jimmy Dorsey rehearsing their numbers. Harry James was also present. And on that day I saw Lena Horne, actress and singer—and one of the most beautiful women I've ever seen. She had a grand voice, and I wanted to be just like her. But, alas, no voice lessons for me—lots of piano though.

Many children in those days took tap dancing and acrobatic lessons. Ginger Rogers and Fred Astaire were popular figures of the time, and my grandfather, commenting on the acrobatics, would say to my parents, "Why are you are spending good money to teach that kid to stand on her head?"

In those days, residence in Hollywood seemed to mean that you were destined to become a director, producer, writer, film editor, actor, or model. I was a model, and I had many photo shoots that took me away from my friends. Those were not my favorite days—being away from my friends.

My piano lessons began at an early age, and Dad was my first teacher. When I was six, my parents decided I needed a professional teacher, and I was turned over to Miss Lock. I remember the first recital. I stood on the stage and announced, "I am going to play THE BEAUTIFUL BLUE DANUBE, and I have had only six lessons" (it was an easy arrangement.) Dad continued to teach me popular pieces of the day. I continued my piano studies in college, and I've been a music and piano teacher all my adult life.

Shakespeare wrote, "All the world 's a stage, And all the men and women merely players: They all have their exits and entrances; and one man in his time plays many parts."

I often think of my life this way. I have vivid recollections of my childhood years—deep and indelible impressions. I think often of all the Blanchard family members who loved me and nurtured me. My warm memories of that early period have helped me work through difficult times in my life. I cherish the Hollywood years, and I've written a letter expressing some thoughts to my beloved Uncle Fred.

A LETTER TO MY UNCLE FRED

*D*ear Uncle Fred:

I wish I could have walked the streets of Los Angeles with you and spent time with you. You had a great sense of humor that was not often apparent to others—but was clearly understood and enjoyed by your family. I lived in your mansion on the Pass, but you were gone by then. Had you been there, we could have walked to the water garden together and talked about all your plans.

My birthday parties were held on your tennis court, and I wish you could have been there. I wish, too, that I could have been with you in San Francisco for the performance of your opera. I would have been so proud of you. It would have been so much fun to have shared the excitement of planning and developing the Hollywood Bowl. I know I could have helped you, and it would have been wonderful to have been there on opening night, sitting next to you and Aunt Grace.

When you built Blanchard Hall, and after that wonderful grand opening, I could have served as the hostess. I would have enjoyed assisting you in all of your cultural endeavors. I've been interested in the cultural arts all my life—part of your legacy to me and to the rest of the family.

Uncle Fred, I have been able to know you in many ways through the family stories. This book is a tribute to you, and through its writing, I feel I have been able to know you even better. I admire you for all of your good works, and I wish from the bottom of my heart that I could have been there with you, celebrating all your achievements and sharing all those memorable times. I think of you each day.

Your loving niece,

Beverly

FREDERICK WOODWARD BLANCHARD

ACHIEVEMENTS—ACTIVITIES— MEMBERSHIPS

Cultural Activities

~ Planned and managed the Blanchard Music and Art Building, also known as Blanchard Hall. The building contained offices and studios for musicians and artists and it housed the first art gallery in Los Angeles. It was the first building west of Chicago devoted exclusively to music and art.

~ Helped found and financially support the Hollywood Bowl. Served as the first president of the Hollywood Bowl Association and was Instrumental in gaining financial backing for the project.

~ Founded and directed the famous Brahms Quintet.

~ Served as president of the American Opera Association.

~ Brought innumerable international musical celebrities to Los Angeles.

~ Served as president of the Los Angeles Symphony Orchestra.

~ Served as president of the Hollywood Art Association.

~ Served as president of the Gamut Club and assisted with its reorganization.

~ Composed "Cosita," a three-act opera performed by the San Francisco Opera Company in 1898.

~ Composed a fiesta march titled "Our Italy."

Civic Activities

~ Served as president of the Broadway Improvement Association. In this capacity, initiated the movement that resulted in giving Los Angeles the first cluster street lights—a system widely adopted around the country.

~ Served as president of the Central Development Association. In this capacity, advanced many applications that compelled the railroads to build Union Plaza Station.

~ Served as chairman of the Union Plaza Station Commission.

~ Served as county chairman and vice president of the first Good Roads Commission in Los Angeles. Initiated legislation that resulted in the development of California's magnificent highway system—one of the first comprehensive systems of paved highways.

~ Founded and organized the Municipal Art Commission, 1906 and served as its first secretary. After charter was granted in 1911, served for eleven years as president.

~ Secured paintings for the new Los Angeles City Hall and helped in the selection of the inscriptions and bronze doors for the building.

~ Served as member of the City Planning Commission.

~ Served as chairman of the budget committee and member of the executive committee of the first Community Chest.

~ Served as head of the Police and Fireman's Relief Fund.

~ Served as chairman of the reception committee for the visit of the King of Belgium. Appointed by King Albert as Officer of the Order of Leopold II, October, 1919.

~ Served as member of the Hollywood Chamber of Commerce.

~ Served as member of the Los Angeles Chamber of Commerce.

~ Served as director/member of the Ventura Boulevard Chamber of Commerce.

~ Served as member of the Hollywood Foothill Association.

~ Served as head of the architectural Board for Windsor Square.

~ Participated in the Arrowhead, Dana Point and Hollywoodland developments.

~ Served as Treasurer of the Businessmen's Cooperative Association.

Memberships

~ Member of the Newport, California, and Catalina Yacht Clubs.

~ Member of the City Club.

~ Member of the Los Angeles Athletic Club.

~ Member of the California Club.

~ Charter member of the Los Angeles Country Club.

NOTES

The information in this book was derived from many sources. The majority of the material and photos came from family records such as scrapbooks, bibles, tapes, diaries, journals, interviews and books.

PHOTO CREDITS

Cover:

Security Pacific Collection/Los Angeles Public Library

    -City Hall

    -Blanchard Hall

HollywoodPhotographs.com

    -Hollywood Bowl

"In Memory of"

HollywoodPhotographs.com

    -FW Blanchard Portrait

Blanchard Family Tree:

Louis Fleckenstein-Los Angeles

    -Portrait of Dudley Blanchard (pg. 9)

Witzel Studios-Los Angeles

    -Portrait of Harry Blanchard (pg. 9)

Chapter 1:

Steckel Studios-Los Angeles

    -Portrait of FW Blanchard (pg. 18)

Chapter 2:

Security Pacific Collection/Los Angeles Public Library

    -Blanchard Hall (pg. 21)

ISBN 141208393-1